Purchased at The Castle,
Smithsonian
May 18, 2007

WASHINGTON, D.C.

THE GROWTH OF THE CITY

WASHINGTON, D.C.

THE GROWTH OF THE CITY

CHARTWELL
BOOKS, INC.

This edition published in 2007 by

CHARTWELL BOOKS, INC.
A Division of
BOOK SALES, INC.
114 Northfield Avenue
Edison, New Jersey 08837

ISBN-13: 978-0-7858-2213-4
ISBN-10: 0-7858-2213-5

Printed and bound in China

Design: Ian Hughes/Compendium Design

Page 2: The monumental marble statue of President Abraham
Lincoln that resides in the Lincoln Memorial at the end of the Mall.
Page 4: Typical of the Neoclassical architecture that dominates
Washington, D.C., the National Archives Building houses some of
the world's most historically significant documents, including the
Constitution of the United States.

Contents

Introduction

The Washington Monument over the Reflecting Pool at dawn. Designed by the prolific Robert Mills, the monument is now the most famous landmark in a city full of famous monuments, though it took a surprising twenty-eight years to build after public donations ran dry and work was suspended for two decades.

Introduction

Situated a short distance inland, about halfway down the East Coast of the United States, on the Potomac River, Washington, D.C. is undoubtedly the most important city in world politics. The seat of the United States' federal government, and home to the president, it is a fascinating metropolis of monuments and grand civic buildings, of imposing architecture and unexpected delights. Built on land chosen by George Washington in 1790, after the end of the American Revolution, and designed specifically to become the capital of the new nation, Washington in the District of Columbia has grown into a dynamic city in its own right in a little over two centuries. With a rich cultural heritage, world-class museums, libraries, and galleries and incorporating the historic port of Georgetown, today's city attracts tourists from around the globe as well as the businesses and institutions that contribute to the Washington's success. Surrounded by the beautiful and tranquil Maryland and Virginia countryside, America's capital is also one of the country's most attractive, and historically significant, cities.

The area that now constitutes the District of Columbia has been inhabited by humans for at least six millennia and possibly as many as twelve. The remnants of three settlements have been unearthed in the immediate vicinity, the most noteworthy being the village of Nacotchanke, home to the Anacostine people. Later, in the seventeenth century, while the English were making their first attempts at colonization downriver at Jamestown, the region's Native-American tribes joined in what is known as the Powhatan Confederacy, lead by the Powhatan, father of the famous Pocahontas. While relations between the tribes and the new settlers were initially cordial, the colonists' brash behavior soon lead to conflict and battles over land rights during the first half of the seventeenth century. By mid-century the Native-Americans were defeated by the British and all but abandoned their villages, moving into the forests inland.

European visits to the Washington area can, in fact, be dated to as early as 1608 and a voyage up the Potomac River by Captain John Smith, if not before. There are maps of the area that predate even this voyage. As the settlement of Jamestown became more firmly established, colonists began to farm the land further upriver, growing tobacco and maize and importing slaves from Africa to work their plantations. By 1660, the farmlands had reached the site that would later become Washington, D.C. During the 1730s a farmer named Augustine Washington built a large mansion fifteen miles to the south of the present day city for himself and his family, which included a son, George. The young boy would eventually inherit the plantation and as the first president of the United States be authorized to choose the site of the new nation's capital. All this was as yet in the future, though by the mid-eighteenth century two

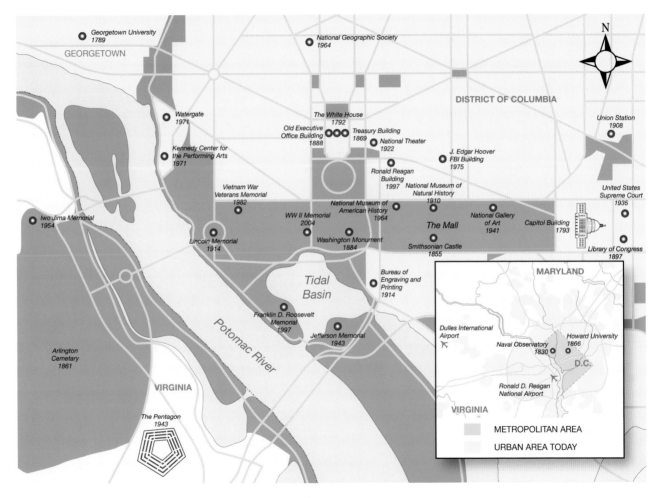

ports were established on opposite banks of the Potomac, which would later be incorporated into the capital; Alexandria and George Town (later to become Georgetown). With tobacco in great demand, rich soil, and no shortage of slave labor, the plantations boomed, and so too did the two towns.

Despite the region's early commercial success, it remained an agricultural area centered upon the transportation hubs of Alexandria and Georgetown until after the end of the War of Independence in 1783. When the Constitution was ratified in 1788, it called for the creation of a seat of government for the fledgling nation. This was to be an independent district, "not exceeding ten square miles," and subject only to Congress. Northern and southern states immediately fell to argument over the site of the future capital, which raged until Secretary of the Treasury Alexander Hamilton and Secretary of State Thomas Jefferson hammered out an arrangement one evening over dinner. Under the agreement,

the war debts of the northern states were to be transferred to the government and, in exchange, the south would become the home of the new capital. The selection of the actual site would be left to President Washington.

The Residence Bill (signed on July 16, 1790) officially granted the president the right to choose the location that while technically in the South was actually close to the center of the nation. The 100

LEFT: This engraving, which dates to 1741, shows slaves working on a typical Virginia tobacco plantation. Sights such as this would have been common up and down the Potomac River.

RIGHT: This late-sixteenth century map was engraved by Theodore de Bry and based on drawings by John White, a prolific artist who journeyed to the early Roanoake Colony with Sir Walter Raleigh. Predating the Jamestown colony, the map is remarkable for its detail and accuracy and also shows Native-American dress and life as well as the feared chief Powhatan.

LEFT: The young George Washington and his family arrived at the Mount Vernon estate in 1736. The original house was built by the future president's father, Augustine, and added to by George. About fifteen miles south of the future site of Washington City, the plantation buildings were typical of their times, featuring a grand house for the plantation owner's family, smaller houses for staff, outbuildings such as stables and kitchens, and, of course, slave quarters.

RIGHT: This map, drawn in 1748 shows the site of the town of Alexandria, which was founded in that year as a transportation hub and inspection center for tobacco. George Town would be established three years later.

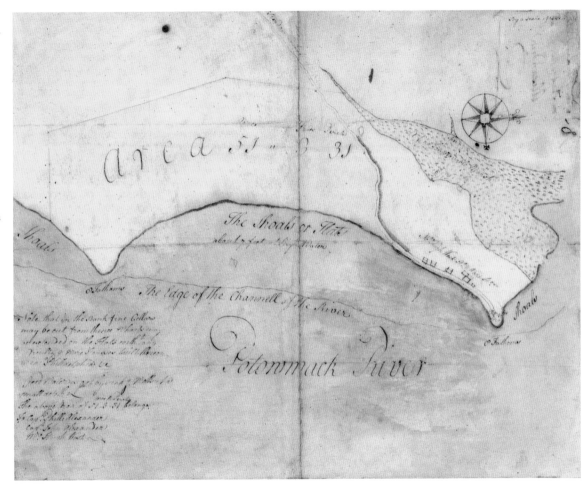

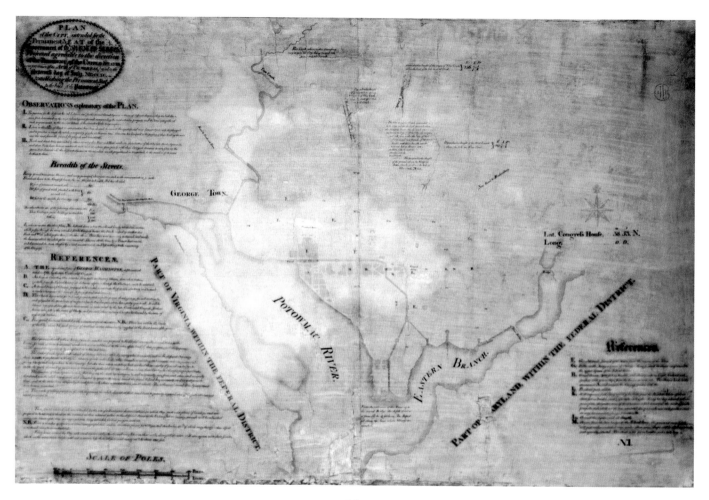

square mile site on the Potomac River that he selected had excellent and established transport in the ports of Georgetown and Alexandria and was also conveniently close to his own estate. On the Maryland side of the river, the new district comprised Washington City and Washington County, while on the Virginia side was Alexandria County. The two states both ceded territory, while Washington himself persuaded local landowners to sell the necessary property to the government. Soon after, Washington tasked the surveyor Andrew Ellicott and his free African-American assistant Benjamin Banneker to survey the district. Many of the stones with which they marked the its boundaries can still be found in place today. The president also accepted the offer of Major Pierre Charles L'Enfant, a French engineer who proposed to design a grand city, a fitting place for the new seat of government. L'Enfant was eventually dismissed due to his stormy relations with local dignitaries and landowners (legend has it that the engineer blew up a house that was in the way of one of his avenues while the owner was out), but his plan was adopted by his successors.

The first city in the United States to be designed in its entirety, L'Enfant's city was arranged on a grid broken by diagonal avenues, with the Capitol Building at the center. Each of the avenues was to be named for a state, and where they crossed imposing circles would be built. Construction work began in 1792 and the first building was, appropriately, the President's House, which would later become known as the White House. The following year, Washington laid the cornerstone of the Capitol Building.

On December 1, 1800, the seat of United States power was formally transferred from Philadelphia to the City of Washington. At the time it was hardly overpopulated, its citizens numbering only about 14,000, including 3,244 slaves. Indeed, with construction still ongoing, it would be decades before Washington could boast a population commensurate with its position as the nation's first city. Growth was further impeded by the war with Britain of 1812, which saw Washington conquered and sacked in 1814. The Treasury, President's House, the Navy Yard, the Capitol, the Arsenal, and War Department were all fired, and the city only escaped being razed to the ground by heavy rainstorms.

Despite this setback, when the war ended Washington's citizens set about making their city anew, as a successful commercial metropolis as well as a striking capital. In 1817, President John Adams and his wife Abigail moved into a new Presidential Mansion (to which the distinctive north and south porticos would be added during the 1820s) and though it would

LEFT: Now faded almost to the point of illegibility, this photograph shows the original 1791 plan of Washington drawn by Major Pierre Charles L'Enfant.

OVER PAGE: Washington from above the Capitol in 1856, showing the Washington Canal, which once ran beside the present day Mall, where Consitution Avenue is now. The canal connected the Capitol Building to the Potomac. It was filled in in 1880, but there remain a few reminders of it existence, such as two lock houses along the Mall, and the name of Canal Street.

remain unfinished until 1829 (and then expanded again during the 1850s), by 1819 Congress were meeting within the Capitol once more. By 1828 work had commenced on the Chesapeake and Ohio Canal, which was intended to provide a trade route to the west, and seven years later the Washington Branch of the Baltimore and Ohio Railroad opened. Many new government buildings were constructed, including many by the prolific architect Robert Mills, including the Treasury (completed in 1842 after the replacement again burned in 1833), Patent Office (1836–67), and the Washington Monument, on which construction commenced in 1848. With many of its government buildings designed in an awe-inspiring Classical Revival style, Washington was beginning to take on its modern appearance.

The city grew steadily, if slowly, in size and prosperity during the years leading up to the Civil War. In 1820, the population stood at 13,247 and by 1860 it was 61,122 (compared to New York's 813,669). However, the tension over racial issues and slavery that were becoming increasingly heated throughout the union were concentrated in the capital, and occasionally boiled over into violence. As demands for the abolition of slavery became louder, Alexandria, an important slave market, requested to return to the

This panoramic view of Washington from above the Potomac dates to 1880. Among the completed sites are the Smithsonian Castle, Botanical Garden, Corcoran Art Gallery, U.S. Treasury, Howard University, Bureau of Engraving and Printing, and the U.S. Post Office. The Washington Monument is still some four years away from completion. L'Enfant's plan for the city is also as yet incomplete, but the city is certainly taking shape.

Virginia, which was a staunch slave state, a request that was granted in 1846. Fifteen years later the slavery question would turn the union against itself during the Civil War. Washington played an active role during the conflict, raising the 50,000 troops of the Army of the Potomac, sheltering wounded soldiers, and helping slaves fleeing the South. In fact, by 1864 the city's population had swelled to over 140,000. When the strife ended, Washington took the lead in the new age, creating the Freedmen's Bureau, which helped African-Americans to find their feet in post slavery America. The bureau also established Howard University in 1867.

In 1871, the District of Columbia was formed from Washington, the County of Washington, and Georgetown. Seven years later the D.C. Organic Act merged all three areas into Washington City. The city's boundaries were now the same as the District of Columbia's. A board of public works was also appointed in 1781 by President Ulysses S. Grant, and began to provide the city with a modern sewer system, paved streets, street lamps, and parks, bankrupting the city for a short while in the process. In 1884, the Washington Monument was finally completed, while in

LEFT: A view over Washington, D.C. in 1916. Note the completed Washington Monument and the recently completed Lincoln Memorial at the end of the Mall.

1889 work began on the Library of Congress. Throughout the city other monuments were erected, parks laid out, schools, homes, museums, and government buildings constructed. The city's future appearance was set forever in 1899 with the passage of the Height of Buildings Act, which prevents the construction of skyscrapers in Washington to this day. As Washington grew more liveable its population increased, reaching 278,718 by the end of the century. By now many middle-class government workers were commuting into the city from suburbs such as Mount Pleasant and LeDroit Park.

As the new century dawned Washington, D.C. reached maturity. The plan proposed by Pierre Charles L'Enfant to President Washington was finally completed under President Theodore Roosevelt in 1901, and work began on the Mall in the same year. Daniel Burnham's famous Union Station opened its doors in 1908. Throughout the remainder of the twentieth century the city continued to grow in step with the status of the United States and improve its infrastructure, notably adding an airport (National in 1940, now known as Ronald Reagan National Airport) and a metro system in 1976. It also cemented its reputation as the heart of United States culture with the opening of numerous museums, galleries, and performing arts venues. As the seat of government, the city has witnessed some of the most profound events of the modern age, from the Civil Rights and Vietnam marches of the fifties and sixties, to the moment when a hijacked passenger jet was deliberately crashed into the Pentagon on September 11, 2001.

Today's Washington, D.C. is a monumental city where government offices, international embassies, and independent political agencies rub shoulders with some of the finest museums and archives in the world as well as the headquarters of world banks and other financial institutions. Around every corner is a monument or building so famous that is familiar to people in every corner of the globe. While it has not been immune to the social problems that have afflicted all western cities over the past decades, Washington, D.C. has done more than most to overcome them and in the twenty-first century the city is a sophisticated place where tourists can visit excellent theaters and intimate neigborhood restaurants and cafés, walk among the cherry trees of the Tidal Basin or picnic in the stunning national parks outside of town. With a metropolitan population of well over half a million from every possible cultural background, it reflects every metropolis in the United States while at the same time being completely, and splendidly, unique.

RIGHT: Drawn just five years later, in 1921, this bird's eye view shows the city in incredible detail. Many buildings and businesses, from Miller's Barber Shop close to the Mall and the Weldit Co. on New Jersey Avenue by Union Station are marked, providing a fascinating glimpse into the 1920s city.

OVER PAGE: This modern photograph taken across the Potomac shows the city at dusk. From left to right the illuminated buildings are: U.S. Capitol, Washington Monument, Lincoln Memorial, and the Jefferson Memorial. Today's Washington, D.C. more than fulfils early visions of a grand and stately city that combines a dignified seat of government with a dynamic city.

WASHINGTON
THE BEAUTIFUL CAPITAL OF THE NATION

Early Days: 1700s–1825

Notwithstanding rebuilding and refurbishment, the White House, at 1600 Pennsylvania Avenue, has been the home of the United States' President since President Adams took residence in 1800.

Early Days: 1700s–1825

The site of Washington, D.C, has been familiar to Europeans since the days of the first English colonies, though the area appears on European maps that even predate Captain John Smith's founding of the Jamestown colony in 1607. However, until the final years of the eighteenth century, the region remained agricultural with its two port and tobacco inspection towns of George Town and Alexandria surrounded by large plantations with grand mansions. All this changed in 1791 when the United States first president, George Washington, named the area as the site of the new nation's future capital. Work began immediately on creating a dignified

model city that would become a worthy seat of government, with Major Pierre L'Enfant supplying a comprehensive plan for the city. The first two buildings to commence construction were the White House and the Capitol Building.

Although government was officially transferred to Washington in 1800, the city was slow to grow. In that year the population stood at just above 3,000 (making it considerably smaller in terms of population than its satellite Alexandria) and only one twentieth the size of New York City. Over the next two and a half decades though the city slowly edged up the list of most populous cities, despite suffering almost complete destruction at the hands of the British in 1814. Population figures for these years can be somewhat misleading as large sections of society would leave the city, making it almost devoid of life, for the summer months. Nevertheless, by 1825 Washington was a small, but rapidly growing metropolis in its own right. More, and grander, houses were being built as people recognized the advantages of living close to the seat of power and some of the buildings and institutions that are so familiar today had their beginnings in these early years.

LEFT: While Surveyors laid out the future streets of Washington, George Town and Alexandria, were already busy ports. This 1795 illustration shows cargo ships docking at Georgetown.

Although there is some argument over whether the Old Stone House at 3051 M Street North-West was built in 1765 or 1767, it is certainly the oldest extant building in Washington. The small, two-storey house is a typical colonial dwelling and is now in the care of the National Park Service.

LEFT: Predating any building in Washington City, Georgetown University was founded in 1789 by John Carroll. The Catholic university has been in operation ever since, though the oldest extant building is the Old North Building, which dates to 1872.

RIGHT: This map shows the area that Washington would occupy before its survey by L'Enfant with the properties of original landowners marked. George Washington himself persuaded each of these men to part with land for the good of the country. At Suter's Fountain Inn, in Georgetown, at the end of March 1790, he offered each $66.67 an acre as well as property in the future city. With negotiations complete, the president dispatched the French-born major to prepare a plan for the city.

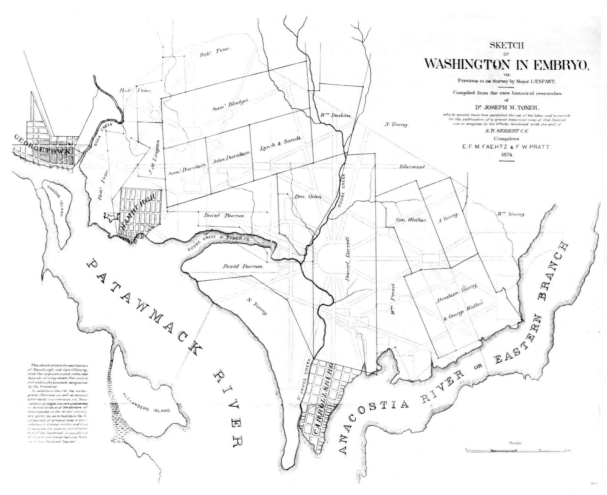

SKETCH
OF
WASHINGTON IN EMBRYO.
VIZ.
Previous to its Survey by Major L'ENFANT.

Compiled from the rare historical researches
of
Dr. JOSEPH M. TONER.
who by special favor has permitted the use of his labor and materials
for the publication of a grand historical map of this District
now in progress by his efforts rendered with the skill of
S.R. SEIBERT C.E.
Compilers
E.F.M. FAEHTZ & F.W. PRATT.
1874.

LEFT: L'Enfant's design is widely considered to be an outstanding work of municipal planning, Although he was influenced by the layout of other cities (particularly the grandest European ones), he devised an original plan for Washington, to which subsequent planners and builders have been largely faithful. Centered on the Capitol Building, which dominates the city from its position on Jenkins Hill the city would feature a "Grand Avenue" (now the Mall) and a Presidential Mansion joined to what L'Enfant called the "Congress House" by a commercial thoroughfare (Pennsylvania Avenue). This map was copied from L'Enfant's original (see page 14), and is from the pen of Andrew Ellicott, George Washington's appointed surveyor.

RIGHT AND OVER PAGE: Perhaps the world's most famous home, the site of the White House (then known simply as the President's House) was chosen by George Washington. The original design was provided by competition winner James Hoban and ground was broken in October 1792. While President Washington took a great interest in the building's progress he never actually lived there himself; that honor went to the second president, John Adams who moved in during 1800. At the time of its completion, the house—like the Capitol Building—was virtually alone on the landscape. The illustration shown here is a plan showing the alterations proposed in 1808 by Benjamin Latrobe. The photographs overleaf show the mansion today and a view of the Oval Office, the president's workspace, which was originally added to the West Wing in 1909, but moved to its current position overlooking the Rose Garden in 1934.

The United States Capitol

After construction began on the President's House, work commenced on a building that would house Congress, with the cornerstone being laid by President Washington in 1793. Its site, atop the plateau of Jenkins Hill was described as, "a pedestal waiting for a monument," by L'Enfant. After a competition to elicit a suitable design ended one further entrant arrived, from a Scottish doctor in the West Indies. The building of Dr. William Thornton's design would occupy the next twenty years and was still unfinished when the British took Washington in 1814 and set the Capitol to the torch.

After the War of 1812, the completion of the Capitol was placed in the hands of Boston architect Charles Bulfinch, who finished the building, with its distinctive copper covered dome, by 1826. Since then, the Capitol has undergone a number of extensions and alterations, notably being fitted with a new dome in 1856 after extension work rendered the scale of the original unsuitable.

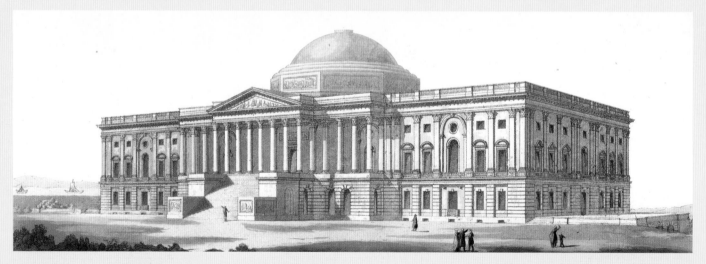

LEFT: This undated engraving shows the building soon after its completion in 1826. Despite the fact that Washington has been the seat of government since the turn of the century, the future city is largely still to be built. At this point in its history Washington was all but empty of citizens, save for politicians, builders, and slaves.

BELOW: Surrounded by building debris and yet to acquire its copper-over-wood dome, this illustration shows the Capitol in 1814, before it was all but destroyed by British forces on the night of August 24.

RIGHT: The capitol receives a new dome during enlargement and refurbishments that took place between 1851 and 1865 under architect Thomas U. Walter.

ABOVE: The National Statuary Hall occupies the chamber that was once the first House chamber and now contains statues of noteworthy citizens from every state.

OVER PAGE: The Capitol today is a symbol of American democracy and continues to house the House of Representatives and the Senate as well as provide museum space and tours for visitors. Although it has been built, rebuilt, altered, restored, and refurbished over more than two centuries, it is an instantly recognizable monument that takes pride of place on L'Enfant's "pedestal."

LEFT: Dating to around 1800, the Sewall-Belmont House is one of the earliest homes to be built in the city. Located opposite the Supreme Court on Constitution Avenue and Second Street, it has been remodeled over the years, but is essentially the same house that has welcomed any number of important political figures over the past two centuries.

RIGHT: Another building that can trace its history to 1800 is Georgetown's grand Dumbarton Oaks mansion. The Federal-style house, which stands in ten acres of outstanding gardens, was commissioned by Maryland senator, William Dorsey.

The Octagon
museum
AMERICAN ARCHITECTURAL FOUNDATION
AMERICAN INSTITUTE OF ARCHITECTS

LEFT: Now a museum of architecture, like the original Capitol Building the Octagon was designed by Dr. William Thornton. Built in 1801 for Colonel John Tayloe III, an intimate of George Washington, the house has a rich political history. It was used as a temporary home by President Madison and his wife Dolley after the White House was burned by British troops in 1814.

RIGHT: This undated painting shows Washington in flames on the night of August 24, 1814. The city was saved from total destruction by a heavy rainstorm that doused the fires, but by the end of the war many buildings that had only recently been completed were in need of either complete rebuilding or extensive restoration. Among those completely or partially destroyed were the Senate and House of Representatives, and Library of Congress (all in the unfinished Capitol), the President's House, the United States Treasury, and Washington Navy Yard. Buildings miraculously saved included the U.S. Patents Office (after Dr. William Thornton, who was working there begged for it to spared) and the offices of the anti-British *National Intelligencer*, where a group of women argued that setting light to it would mean the burning of many homes.

LEFT: St. John's Episcopal Church was built in 1816 by Benjamin Latrobe. Known as "the Church of the Presidents," every president since James Madison has worshiped here. It was also the site of Patrick Henry's famed "Give me liberty or give me death" speech.

RIGHT: Another building designed by Dr. Thornton, is Georgetown's Tudor Place, which was built for the grand-daughter of Martha Washington and her husband. Completed in 1816, the building is in the grand Federal Style that marks so much of the city's architecture and includes an interesting domed portico over the entrance.

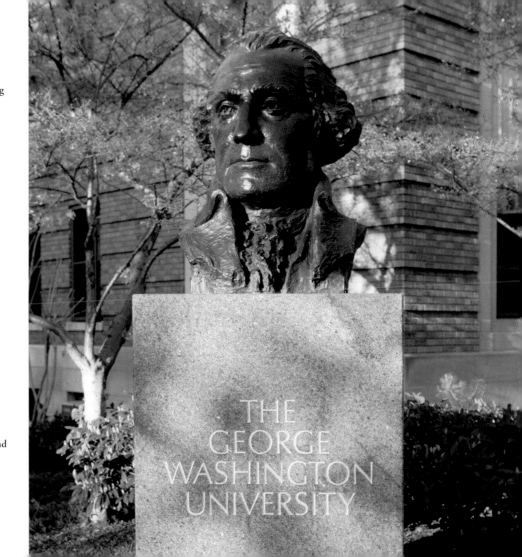

r: A hostelry has stood at this location at 1401
asylvania Avenue since 1816. Purchased by Henry
ard, in 1850, the hotel has since welcomed every U.S.
dent in opulent style. The present Beaux Arts building
s to 1904.

IT: Founded in 1821 as the Columbian College on land
ated by the former president, George Washington
versity has grown to become the city's foremost
ersity. Only a short distance from the Mall and the
te House, it was renamed in honor of President
hington in 1904.

LEFT AND RIGHT: The U.S. Botanic Garden dates back to the earliest days of the city. It was created by Congress in 1824 in order to cultivate plant species that might prove of use to the nation. Over subsequent years the gardens have been enlarged and renovated, most notably in 1842 with the addition of species brought back from the South Seas by the Wilkes Expedition, in 1933 when the Palm House was built, and more recently with additional grounds being set aside for a Water Garden, Showcase Garden, and a Rose Garden. The photographs show the gardens at the foot of Capitol Hill circa 1865 and the eighty-foot-high Palm House shortly after its 1933 opening.

RIGHT AND LEFT: Originally part of the White House grounds, Lafayette Square was named for the Revolutionary War hero in 1824. St. John's Church is on the square, as are a number of fine eighteenth century homes. Statuary within the park celebrates some of the most significant participants in the War of Independence, including the Marquis himself (RIGHT) and Andrew Jackson (LEFT).

The Heart of the Union: 1826–65

This view of Washington, which dates to 1838, is taken from Arlington House (now in Arlington National Cemetery). The city is growing slowly, though many of the most populated residential areas are in the older area of Georgetown. The city is dominated by the copper-domed Capitol Building.

The Heart of the Union: 1826–65

In the years leading up to the Civil War, Washington began to increase more rapidly in size and population, though it was during the war years that it experienced its most dramatic expansion. A concerted effort to establish the city as commercially successful in its own right, rather than as merely a metropolis of government offices, led to the building of the Chesapeake & Ohio Canal while the capital also welcomed its first railroad line, joining it to Baltimore. Stores and businesses sprang up along the city's main commercial thoroughfare, Pennsylvania Avenue. Impressive government buildings were raised, modeled on the architecture of Ancient Greece, the birthplace of civilization and democracy, and efforts commenced on landscaping the city, notably in 1850 when Andrew Jackson Downing began work on the Mall. The years before the war also saw the birth of the Smithsonian Institute and the building of the Smithsonian castle, now at the heart of a huge museum and gallery complex.

Official census figures put Washington's population at 18,826 in 1830. By 1860, with war brewing, the number of citizens had increased to 61,122. During the war that figure would double, with some sources suggesting that 140,000 people were resident in the capital. Unprepared for such a deluge, Washington struggled to house the new arrivals, who included soldiers called upon to defend the capital and fleeing slaves from the south, but when the conflict ended, the population dwindled slightly, though it was now well in excess of 100,000 and rising rapidly. The city was about to enter an unparalleled period of growth and building.

LEFT AND RIGHT: Work on the Chesapeake & Ohio Canal commenced in 1828. It was intended as a commercial artery linking the Potomac and Ohio rivers and was funded by the towns along the Potomac and Chesapeake Bay that stood to benefit from it. Nevertheless, building was slow and the canal eventually rendered obsolete by the railroad, but in 1971 it was designated a national park and is now a beautiful stretch of water that travels through some of Washington's most historic districts and most stunning countryside.

Founded in 1830 as the Depot of Charts and Instruments, the U.S. Naval Observatory was built in 1842. Originally positioned far from the city (as can be seen in this pastoral photograph dating to the late 1860s), Washington has grown up around it.

The Baltimore & Ohio Railroad reached Washington in 1835 with a terminal at Second and Pennsylvania Avenue North West, close to the Capitol. Over the coming decades the rail network would gradually spread across the United States, connecting the capital with the nation and bringing goods and passengers into the city.

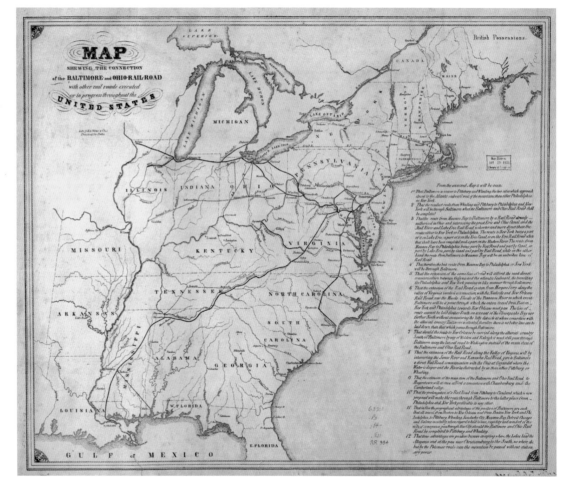

LEFT: The construction of the present Treasury Building, designed by Robert Mills, began in 1836 after a previous building (by White House architect James Hoban) was burned by arsonists. That building had itself replaced a structure that was burned by the British in 1814. Curiously, the first building had also succumbed to flames in 1801 and needed extensive repairs. This building has so far resisted fire and has served the nation since the first wings were occupied in 1839.

RIGHT: Another building designed by Robert Mills and begun in 1836 was the Patent Office. The similarities between the two, with their Classical porticoes and Palladian symmetry, are remarkable. Indeed, Mills modeled the porticoes on the Parthenon in Greece. The building took thirty-one years to complete and now houses the Smithsonian American Art Museum and the National Portrait Gallery.

The Washington Monument

The idea of a monument to honor the achievements of George Washington stretch back to the time of the First Continental Congress, though Congress failed to act on the plan. In fact, the fund for the building work was eventually raised by public subscription between 1833 and 1847. With a design by Robert Mills accepted, work began on the obelisk in 1848. The cornerstone was laid on July 4 of that year with the trowel used by Washington to lay the cornerstone of the Capitol Building called into service. Though construction began well, by 1854 work was halted by arguments over the building standards, lack of funds, and then the Civil War. In fact, it was twenty-five years until work began again, this time funded by the government. The capstone was finally set in place on December 6, 1884. Complete, the Washington Monument became the tallest structure in the world.

LEFT: Mills original design for the monument included a colonnaded temple at the base and martial statuary.

RIGHT: This early photograph shows the incomplete monument as it appeared for twenty-five years until President Grant approved funds for completion.

The Washington Monument is still the tallest structure in the city and is an integral part of the skyline as much as the Statue of Liberty is in New York. The top of the monument can be reached by stairs or elevator and observation windows provide stunning views out over the city and surrounding countryside.

LEFT: The narrow, mile long length of the Mall, which stretches between the Capitol and the Washington Monument is probably the world's most recogized and photographed park. Although provision was made for a "Grand Avenue" in L'Enfant's original plan, landscaping work did not begin until 1850 and was stopped soon after when money ran out. The park was finally completed after the Civil War and is now lined by the greatest collection of museums and galleries in the world.

RIGHT: This 1860 painting provides a glimpse of how Washington's main commercial thoroughfare appeared shortly before the advent of war. It shows the telegraph office and the National Hotel, at Pennsylvania and Sixth Street, North-West, as carriages move up and down Pennsylvania Avenue.

Designed by James Renwick, Jr., the Renwick Gallery forms a part of the Smithsonian American Art Museum and dates back to 1858.

LEFT AND RIGHT: The black and white photograph shows a view over Independence Avenue to the Smithsonian Castle in 1865, ten years after completion. Note how sparsely built up the heart of the city is almost a century after President Washington selected the site. The Smithsonian is unusual in Washington, D.C. for breaking with the monumental Federal architectural style. Instead it is a superb example of Victorian Gothic by James Renwick, who also designed New York's St. Patrick's Cathedral. The Smithsonian was founded with a huge legacy from English scientist James Smithson, who willed his fortune to create a center of knowledge in the United States despite never having set foot in the country.

LEFT: During the Civil War, Washington was busier than at any point during its history and John T. Ford built this theater in 1863 to entertain the new citizens who flooded into the city (this photograph was taken soon after its completion). Tragically, it would become infamous just two years later when President Lincoln was assassinated here by John Wilkes Booth. Deserted by audiences, Ford's Theatre was derelict for almost a century, but has now been fully restored and is a working theater once more. It also commemorates the president who died here.

ABOVE: Arlington National Cemetery has a long history that stretches back to the Custis family. George Washington Parke Custis (the adopted son of George Washington) built the first house here which eventually became the property of Colonel Robert E. Lee. The estate was seized when Lee left to serve the Confederate Army, and was designated a cemetery in 1864. Among the famous graves and memorials here now are the tomb of Pierre L'Enfant, and John F. Kennedy whose grave is marked by an eternal flame that was lit by his wife Jackie during his funeral. The cemetery also contains the garaves of over a quarter of a million U.S. veterans.

Washington at War

Historically, Washington has experienced its greatest spurts of growth during national crises, as more jobs are usually created by a government expanding to deal with the problem. The first such emergency was the Civil War. Not only did the government itself expand, but between 1861 and 1865 tens of thousands of troops were stationed here to protect the capital of the Union. Numerous camps and forts were built for military personnel and people flocked to the city from across the country to participate in the war effort. Escaping slaves from the South also sought sanctuary here, particularly after slavery was abolished in the District of Columbia in 1862. In fact, over the course of the war Washington's population doubled to about 140,000.

RIGHT: Most famously used as a gaol for Confederate prisoners during the Civil War, the Old Capitol Prison at First and A streets North-East was built in 1800 and housed Congress for over a decade after the Capitol was burned in 1814.

LEFT: Taken by renowned Civil War photographer Matthew Brady, this photograph shows a Washington park full of six-pounder Wiard guns being inspected by General David E. Sickles.

LEFT: During the Civil War Washington also served as a hospital city, treating wounded men brought back from the front. This photograph shows hospital tents behind Douglas Hospital.

RIGHT: While time has not been kind to this photograph, it is a fascinating document of Civil War Washington, with citizens on Pennsylvania Avenue watching mounted officers and infantrymen while a band plays.

LEFT: Throughout the Civil War Washington was protected by a ring of forts, including Fort Stevens, shown here. It was here that President Lincoln came under fire while visiting during the Battle of Fort Stevens, which took place on July 11 and 12, 1864.

RIGHT: On the evening of April 14, 1865, just five days after the surrender of General Lee at Appomattox, President Lincoln was assassinated. His body was carried to a train and taken west to Oak Ridge Cemetery in Springfield, Illinois. This photograph shows the funeral procession on Pennsylvania Avenue.

City Beautiful: 1866–1913

Washington, D.C as it appeared in 1901, the year that L'Enfant's plan was finally completed and Senator James McMillan proposed the "City Beautiful" plan.

City Beautiful: 1866–1913

These five decades saw Washington evolve at a much more rapid rate than previously and become recognizably the city of today. A public works board under the charge of Alexander Robey Shepherd, known simply as "Boss," began a series of civic improvements from 1871 onward. Where the vastly enlarged population had previously lived in a city of mud streets, devoid of a sewer system save the stinking Washington Canal, now the city's thoroughfares were graded and sidewalks lit by streetlamps. Water and sewer systems were built and public transport (by horse-drawn trolley) commenced. While Washington quickly became a more liveable city, the Boss bankrupted it in the process. Nevertheless, by 1901 Le'Enfant's original plan was finally deemed complete, and in the same year Senator James McMillan's City Beautiful plan also began a series of works aimed at beautifying the city, particularly the core around the Mall.

Some of the city's most remarkable, and imposing, buildings and sights date to these decades, including the Jefferson Building of the Library of Congress, the Old Post Office, the National Zoo, Tidal Basin, and Union Station as well as parks, walkways, bridges, sculptures , and monuments. The Washington Monument was also

finally completed in 1884 (it is still possible to see the contrast in the color of the stones where building was stopped for twenty-five years). With public transport also came a population shift toward new suburbs.

LEFT: Center Market on Pennsylvania Avenue between Seventh and Ninth opened in 1871 and was the largest of the city's markets as well as its most popular.

ABOVE: Seen here with the U.S. Botanical Garden in the background the Bartholdi Fountain was created by the sculptor of the Statue of Liberty for the 1876 Centennial.

This five-part panorama shows the Mall area of Washington and surrounding buildings, from the Smithsonian Castle in 1879. The left section shows Washington Monument under construction in background, with Agriculture Department at left. The left center and center sections show the B Street (now Constitution Avenue) side of the Mall with building trade structures and Center Market. The right center section shows Baltimore and Potomac Railroad station and tracks. The right section includes the U.S. Capitol in the background and Independence Avenue area of Capitol Hill.

ABOVE: These Georgetown rowhouses date to the 1880s. The latter decades of the nineteenth century saw a great rise in Washington's population (almost 150,000 by 1880 and over 230,000 by the beginning of the 1890s), and many residences around the city were built around this time. The city also had a large number of impoverished citizens who lived in tucked away alleys around the city.

ABOVE: This view of Washington dates to 1886 and shows pedestrians and carriages on the site that would shortly be excavated to make way for the Library of Congress.

Designed by Montgomery C. Meigs and completed in 1887, this ornate and flamboyant building was the home of the Pension Bureau. The Great Hall, seen here, is 316 feet by 116 feet with its ceiling reaching 159 feet above the floor. The huge Corinthian columns are each twenty-five feet in circumference. Since 1980 the building has been home to the National Building Museum.

LEFT: The Dwight D. Eisenhower Executive Office building is another of Washington's structures that drew criticism in its break from the city's Neoclassical tradition. Built in the French Second Empire style, popular at the time the building opened in 1888, it is close to the White House and the home of the Vice President's office.

BELOW: Landscaped by the famous Frederick Law Olmsted, designer of New York's Central Park, Washington's National Zoological Park opened in 1891, having been relocated from its original site on the Mall.

The Tidal Basin was created in 1897 to help control flooding of the Potomac. Since then the expanse of water has become an integral part of the Washington cityscape, surrounded by monuments, such as the Jefferson Memorial seen here. The cherry trees that surround it were a gift from Japan in 1912.

The Library of Congress

The Library of Congress is one of the world's foremost repositories of learning spread across three buildings each of which is a superb architectural feat in its own right. Founded in 1800, the original library was housed in the Capitol Building, but was totally destroyed when the building was put to the flame by the British in 1814. The replacement library was begun by Thomas Jefferson who sold his own library of 6,487 books to Congress for $23,940 in 1815. The library moved into the first of its present three homes in 1897. Known as the Thomas Jefferson Building, the exquisite building was designed by architects John L. Smithmeyer and Paul J. Pelz.

ABOVE: Dated 1880, this tattered photograph shows the excavated site of the future library on Capitol Hill.

ABOVE AND RIGHT:
These images show
construction progress.
The cornerstone of the
building was laid on
August 28, 1890 and the
final stone of the
superstructure was in
place by July 7, 1894.
Nevertheless completing
the internal features,
sculptures, and murals
took almost as long as
the building work itself.
The building was finally
opened on November 1,
1897.

ABOVE: The completed Thomas Jefferson Building of the Library of Congress shortly after its 1897 completion.

RIGHT: Constructed with white Italian marble and featuring statues of the goddess Minerva by Herbert Adams, the Great Hall of the Library of Congess is a dizzying architectural achievement. High above the marble floor, with its brass inlay, light streams through art glass skylights. Around the walls on the west wall are bronze masks that once provided drinking water.

LEFT: Originally housed in the Renwick Gallery, the expanding collection of William Wilson Corocan required a larger space toward the end of the nineteenth century. The Corocan Gallery of Art opened in 1897 and was designed to house the huge collection of American works by Ernest Flagg.

ABOVE: This photograph shows a baseball game between Philadelphia and Washington at American League Park in 1900. The ballpark was located at the corner of Florida Avenue and Trinidad Avenue, NE and was the home of the Washington Senators from 1901 to 1903 when the team moved to the site that would eventually become Griffith Stadium.

LEFT AND RIGHT: Like the Smithsonian Castle, the magnificent Romanesque architecture of the Old Post Office with its awe-inspiring hall, is somewhat at odds with its Neoclassical Washington neighbors. For that reason it has often been the subject of controversy and has escaped demolition through a combination of luck and the efforts of preservationists. Built in 1899, the building housed the post office until 1934, but has now been converted to retail and recreation space.

At around the turn of the century Washington was developing suburbs as streetcar and rail lines allowed workers to travel quickly and easily beyond the city center. The most prestigious was Kalorama, which is located north of the Dupont Circle. The photograph shows the view to the suburb over the Taft Bridge.

LEFT AND RIGHT: Construction work began on Washington National Cathedral on September 29, 1907 with the laying of a cornerstone than contained a stone from a field in Bethlehem, and continued for most of the twentieth century. In fact, it was not until the west towers were finished in 1990 that building was completed, though services have been conducted in the Bethlehem Chapel since 1912.

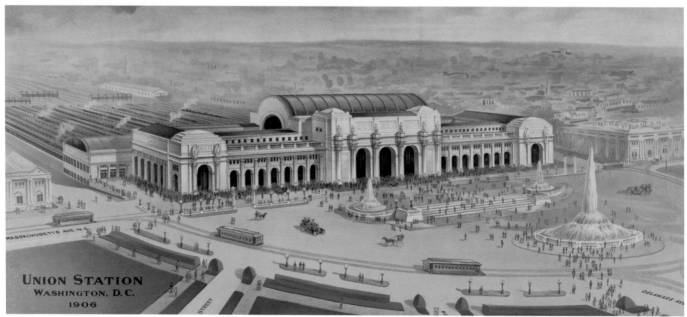

UNION STATION
WASHINGTON, D.C.
1906

Union Station is the masterpiece of architect Daniel Burnham. When completed in 1908, it was the largest train station anywhere. Built on the site of a former shanty town, Union Station was designed in a grand Beaux Arts style with lofty barrel-vaulted ceilings featuring twenty-two karat gold leaf. Among its conveniences were a monogramming shop, Turkish bath, high-class restaurant, and a mortuary.

Despite its magnificence, Union Station suffered during the age of air travel until the 1980s when a massive conservation project restored the building to its former glory. Still a working station, it now also houses shops, cafes, and restaurants and is one of the most popular tourist destinations in the city.

LEFT: Taken around 1910, this photograph of Pennsylvania Avenue at Eleventh Street is a stark contrast to the Civil War photo of Pennsylvania Avenue (on page 77) taken just four and a half decades previously. The trim streets are testament to the City Beautiful campaign, a reform movement, which from 1901 sought to beautify the city as much in an attempt to prevent social decay as for any aesthetic reasons.

RIGHT: Despite the City Beautiful campaign, not all of Washington's citizens lived in sanitary and safe conditions. This photograph shows a roughly constructed alley close to the Capitol that would have been inhabited by the city's poorest inhabitants.

LEFT: Taken around the same date as the previous photograph, this image is captioned, "N. side of F Street between 6th & 7th N.W." Electric streetcar services had been running in the capital since the 1890s and were responsible for the development of new suburban neighborhoods that could now be easily reached by commuters.

RIGHT AND BELOW: Part of the Smithsonian Institution complex of museums and facilities along the Mall, the National Museum of Natural History opened its doors to the public in 1910. Comprising 1.5 million square feet of floor space beneath its green-domed roof, the museum includes over 125 million specimens.

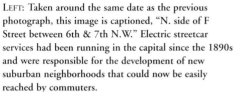

War and Peace: 1914–45

War and Peace: 1914–45

Over the next three and a half decades Washington was at the political center of two world wars and the catastrophe of the Great Depression. Despite the national and local struggles, the capital continued to expand, sometimes at a dizzying pace, most notably during the difficult thirties when almost 200,000 new citizens came to live in the city and again during World War II when the population exceeded a million for the first time. As during the Civil War, many of the latter new Washingtonians were connected with the war effort—in times of emergency and turmoil the capital is always busier. In fact, people were arriving at such a rate that from 1940 the District of Columbia was approving over 1,500 building permits each month and even then many were forced to live in temporary buildings. Government spilled out of its imposing temples of architecture and into prefabs along the Mall.

Construction of the city as we know it today continued apace. Though somewhat scaled down in response to the Great Depression, the vast complex of governmental buildings of the Federal triangle were completed in the thirties, while the U.S. Supreme Court finally found a home of its own in 1935. The Federal Reserve Building and Folger Shakespeare Library also date to this period along with many other fine works of architecture, landscaping, and public sculpture. Meanwhile, new monuments also appeared throughout a city conscious of its position as the repository of American memory and experience. Great presidents to receive memorials during this period include Lincoln, Grant, and Jefferson.

RIGHT AND PREVIOUS PAGE: The Lincoln Memorial is built on land that was once so marshy that it needed to be drained before construction could begin. Designed by Henry Bacon and built in 1914, the Classical-inspired monument to one of the United States' greatest presidents features a huge statue of Lincoln in marble and thirty-six Doric columns. Carved into the south wall are the immortal words of Lincoln's Gettysburg Address.

BELOW: Also dating to 1914, the home of the U.S. Bureau of Engraving and Printing was designed by James Knox Taylor. The bureau was created in 1863 to produce standard currency for the United States.

RIGHT: Conforming to L'Enfant's plan of grand circles, each of which would honor great Americans, Dupont Circle, to the northwest of the White House, celebrates Admiral Samuel Francis, naval hero of the Civil War. In 1921, the current fountain at the center replaced a bronze statue that was donated by the admiral's family.

Designed by the great architectural firm of McKim, Mead & White and built during the 1920s, the low, Neoclassical Memorial Bridge is symbolic of the link between North and South. In crossing the Potomac it connects the Lincoln Memorial to the Robert E. Lee Memorial in Arlington.

LEFT: About halfway between the White House and Union Station, Washington's Chinatown is a popular, bustling area despite its relatively small size. The area became a distinctively Chinese area in about 1930 and the "Friendship Gate," a gift from sister city Beijing, was erected in 1986.

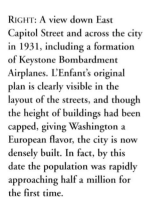

RIGHT: A view down East Capitol Street and across the city in 1931, including a formation of Keystone Bombardment Airplanes. L'Enfant's original plan is clearly visible in the layout of the streets, and though the height of buildings had been capped, giving Washington a European flavor, the city is now densely built. In fact, by this date the population was rapidly approaching half a million for the first time.

LEFT: An aerial view of the Federal Triangle in 1934, Bounded by Fifteenth Street and Constitution Avenue (running down the left of the photograph) the government building unit measures ten blocks long and five blocks on its base. The group of new buildings was authorized by the Coolidge administration and was nearing completion under the Roosevelt regime at the time this photo was taken. In the foreground, forming the base of the triangle, is the department of Commerce building, situated on Fifteenth Street. Along the side (Constitution Avenue), looking toward the apex of the triangle are, successively, the Interstate Commerce, Internal Revenue, Justice, and Archives Buildings. Looking from the base along Pennsylvania Avenue are the Customs Building, the new Post Office and the old Post Office

RIGHT: Donated to the nation by Henry Clay Folger and opened in 1932, the Folger Shakespeare Library houses the world's greatest collection of Shakespeare's works, including a number of rare First Folios. The library also contains a small theater that stages performances of Shakespeare's plays in a recreated Elizabethan environment.

Another of Washington's splendid Palladian porticoes, that belonging to the U.S. Supreme Court is particularly impressive and owes its design to Cass Gilbert. Opened in 1935, the steps leading up to the entrance are watched over by two sculptures: Guardian of the Law and Contemplation of Justice.

The National Gallery of Art was founded in 1936 when philanthropist Andrew Mellon donated his art collection to the nation and also offered to finance a building to house it. The result was this beautiful building, designed in Washington's favourite Neoclassical style by architect John Russell Pope. The new museum opened its doors to the public in 1941.

The work of architect Paul Philippe Cret, the Federal Reserve Building opened in 1937. As its name suggests, the bank regulates financial reserves for banks in twelve districts across the nation.

The Pentagon is actually across the Potomac from Washington in Arlington, Virginia, but as one of the great symbols of U.S. power is very much a part of the capital's landscape. Dedicated on January 15, 1943, the headquarters of the U.S. Department of Defense remains the largest office building in the world.

The Thomas Jefferson Memorial on the south bank of the Tidal Basin was also designed by John Russell Pope and dedicated in 1943. The domed and colonnaded building contains a nineteen foot bronze statue of the great man.

LEFT AND RIGHT: Watched by President Roosevelt, who had selected its site, National Airport was officially opened on June 16, 1941. The epitome of chic modern design that also contained elements of Washington's pervasive Neoclassicism, the airport caused some wrangling about whether it came under the jurisdiction of Virginia or the District of Columbia, since it was built on landfill in the Potomac that had not previously existed. The final compromise put the airport in Virginia but gave the district control over it. Its name was changed to honor former President Ronald Reagan in 1998. The black and white photograph shows inspection of a Boeing B-29 Superfortress during wartime in 1944.

Modern Washington: 1946–Today

Modern Washington: 1946–Today

Since World War II, Washington has continued to grow adding new buildings such as the Kennedy Center, Hirshhorn Museum and Sackler Gallery to the cityscape as well as constructing a new Metro system and continuing to honor America's heroes, whether they be great presidents such as Franklin D. Roosevelt or soldiers who have given their lives on battlefields around the world.

As the United States of America has grown as a superpower, so its capital city has come to reflect its dominance of world politics. Modern Washington is a place where new and colossal buildings such as the Watergate Complex and Ronald Reagan Building rub shoulders with two hundred years of heritage. Today's Washington, D.C. is a city that is undoubtedly greater than the sum of its parts, though those parts include an incredible range of museums, galleries, public spaces, important architecture, and public monuments. While its population is many times smaller than the country's biggest cities, Washington receives a disproportionate amount of visitors and is as sophisticated and elegant as any world metropolis. The 1899 capping of building heights to thirteen stories has also resulted in a city that despite its importance has the feel of a more intimate and European city of vistas.

PREVIOUS PAGE: Washington, D.C. in the twenty-first century successfully combines its role as the United States' capital and a center of heritage with a modern dynamism.

RIGHT: Honoring Andrew Mellon, whose generous donation of artworks provided the National Gallery with its first collection, the Mellon Fountain adds Classical elegance to the space in front of the museum. Funded by a group of the philanthropist's friends, the fountain was dedicated in 1952.

City of Protest

Since Coxey's Army arrived in 1894 to raise awareness of unemployment, Washington has been visited many times by groups of people wishing to exercise their democratic right to protest. Groups as diverse as Women's Suffrage and the Ku Klux Klan have all marched on the capital to make their point. During the latter decades of the twentieth century, the city witnessed some of the largest mass demonstrations in history culminating in the National Mobilization to End the War of November 15, 1969, which brought 600,000 protestors onto Washington's streets.

RIGHT: Reverend Martin Luther King, Jr. waves to participants in the Civil Rights Movement's March on Washington from the Lincoln Memorial. It was from this spot that he delivered his famous "I Have a Dream" speech on August 28, 1963.

Protestors of the Vietnam War at the Peace Moratorium on the Mall in Washington, D.C. on November 15, 1969. The Peace Moratorium is believed to have been the largest demonstration in U.S. history.

Tens of thousands of protesters joined the "Million Mom March" in Washington, May 14, 2000, to demand that Congress pass "common sense gun control" and try to stem the gun violence that claims more than 30,000 American lives a year.

LEFT: Dedicated in 1954, the Iwo Jima Memorial commemorates the raising of the United States flag over Mount Suribachi in Iwo Jima, and honors the Marines who took part in the World War II conflict with Japan.

RIGHT: The John F. Kennedy Center is a vast performance space that comprises an opera house, theater, and concert hall. Designed by Edward Durrell Stone, the center opened in 1971 and was named for the president who took an active role in raising funds for the building, though he never lived to see it completed.

LEFT: The notorious site of a 1972 break-in that led to the resignation of President Nixon, the Watergate Complex is the neighbor of the Kennedy Center and was completed in 1971.

RIGHT: A part of the Smithsonian Institution, the Hirshhorn Museum opened its controversial doors in 1974. As was intended, its uncompromising modern architecture elicits strong responses, but there is no doubting that it is a worthy exhibition space for the vast collection of contemporary art that it houses.

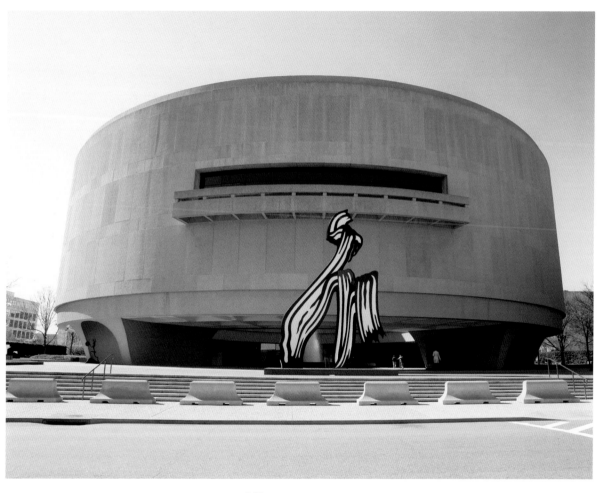

BELOW: Dedicated in 1975, the J. Edgar Hoover FBI Building is constructed of poured concrete and designed in the "Brutalist" style. As controversial as the former FBI director for whom it is named, the building featured in *Washingtonian* magazine's "Buildings I'd Tear Down."

RIGHT: An important 1976 addition to the city was the Metro system, which has since grown to include five lines comprising over a 100 miles of track with eighty-six stations. Much of the system's architecture was designed by Harry Weese and is well-known for its heavy use of geometric and unadorned concrete motifs.

The largest museum of its kind in the world, the National Air and Space Museum opened in 1976 in a spectacular building by Hellmuth, Obata, and Kassabaum. This photograph shows the *Spirit of St. Louis*, in which Charles Lindbergh made the first solo transatlantic flight in 1927.

THEY (WHO) SEEK TO ESTABLISH
SYSTEMS OF GOVERNMENT BASED ON
THE REGIMENTATION OF ALL HUMAN
BEINGS BY A HANDFUL OF INDIVIDUAL
RULERS... CALL THIS A NEW ORDER.
IT IS NOT NEW AND IT IS NOT ORDER.

LEFT: At the heart of a grand memorial park dedicated to the former president on the shore of the Tidal Basin, is the superb sculpture of Franklin Delano Roosevelt with his dog Fala by Neil Estern. Comprising four open-air "rooms," the park contains sculptures and reliefs that depict key moments from Roosevelt's presidency as well as waterfalls that symbolize his commitment to peace. It was completed in 1997.

RIGHT: Designed by a twenty-one year old student, Maya Lin, and completed in 1982, the Vietnam Veterans Memorial Wall consists of two pieces of black granite, each 246 feet nine inches long, upon which are inscribed the names of those who either died or were classified as missing in action during the conflict.

Dedicated on July 27, 1995, the Korean War Veterans Memorial honors those who fought in what has been called America's "forgotten war." The emotive memorial consists of nineteen statues of patrolling soldiers making their way toward the United States flag.

FAR LEFT: At over three million square feet, the Ronald Reagan Building is a vast complex that contains public, trade, and government spaces. Designed by Pei, Cobb, Freed & Partners and completed in 1997, the Ronald Reagan Building takes its inspiration from Classical architecture and complements its Washington surroundings.

LEFT: An aerial view of the U.S. capital city today, looking northeast toward the Washington Monument, Tidal Basin, and Jefferson Memorial. The Capitol Dome can be made out in the center left.

RIGHT: Created by an Act of Congress in 1989, the National Museum of the American Indian is the sixteenth Museum of the Smithsonian Institution and the first institution devoted to Native-American life and culture. The distinctive museum with its Kasota limestone covered walls was designed to resemble a wind-eroded rock formation. It opened in 2004.

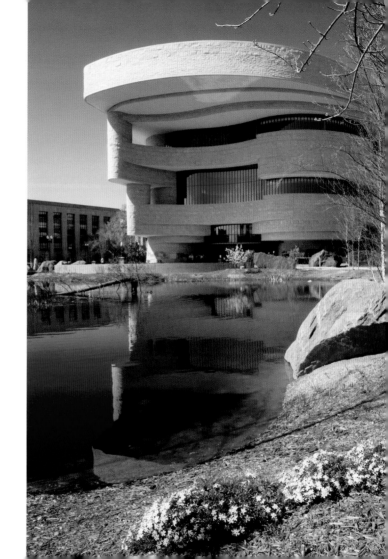

The National World War II Memorial is a beautifully designed tribute to those Americans who fell during the 1939-45 conflict. Centered on the Rainbow Pool, the memorial is rich in symbolism and remembrance including a "Field of Stars." Each of the 4,000 stars on this wall commemorates 1,000 servicemen who gave their lives.

In little more than two centuries since L'Enfant drew up his grand plan for Washington the city has grown to occupy a vast urban sprawl that stretches well beyond the limits of the District of Columbia and is centered on a monumental city that has faithfully stuck to the French major's design.